The Puffin's Advice

Drawings and Verse
by Simon Drew

A BOOK FOR THE SINGLE OR
THE MARRIED OR THOSE THINKING
OF CHANGING FROM
ONE TO THE OTHER.

Antique Collectors' Club

To my wife, Caroline

© 1989 Simon Drew
World copyright reserved
First published 1989
ISBN 1-85149-102-3

British Library CIP data
Drew, Simon
    The Puffin's Advice
I. Title
821'.914

Published and printed in England by the Antique Collectors' Club Ltd., Woodbridge, Suffolk.

FOREWORD

The Puffin's Advice that follows is told in words and pictures in such a way that every main illustration contains an item that is somehow concealed in the accompanying text (where it may span two words or be incorrectly spelt).
For instance the hat on this page is taken from the fourth word of the sentence above.

However this is only an incidental diversion and is in no way an essential part of the 'Advice'.

(If you would like a list of the hidden items write to me at 13 Foss St. Dartmouth.)
S.D.

3

A robin was once in love with a wren:
they wanted to marry but didn't know when.

So they went to a puffin to ask his advice.
He said to them: "Listen, I won't say this twice:

wait till you see a thrush in a stocking,

and naked mute swans
(but don't find it shocking),

and when you find avocets drinking brown ale,

and light fingered parrots that end up in jail,

and when there are lapwings that fly round
the earth,
and carry a ruler
to measure
its
girth,

11

and when all the pheasants are made into soup,

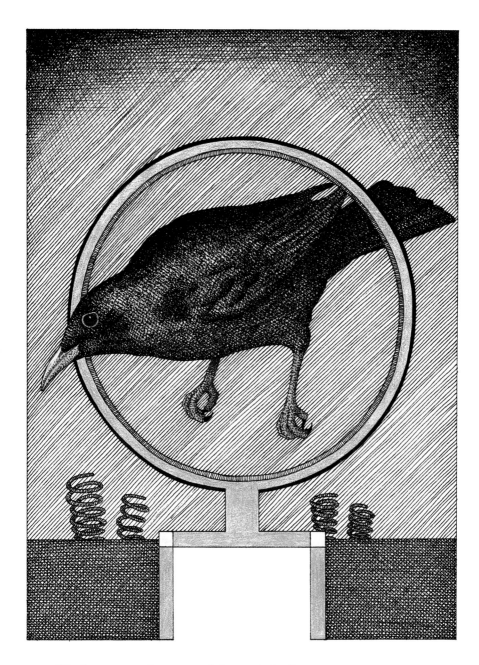

you'll know that a blackbird
can spring through a hoop;

and when you discover a miserly chough
that's counting its cash . . .

. . . and it's never enough,

when there are wheels on the legs of a stork,

and spoonbills have learnt how to eat with a fork,

and when there's a shoveler rooting up trees
while seeking its purse that it lost with its keys,

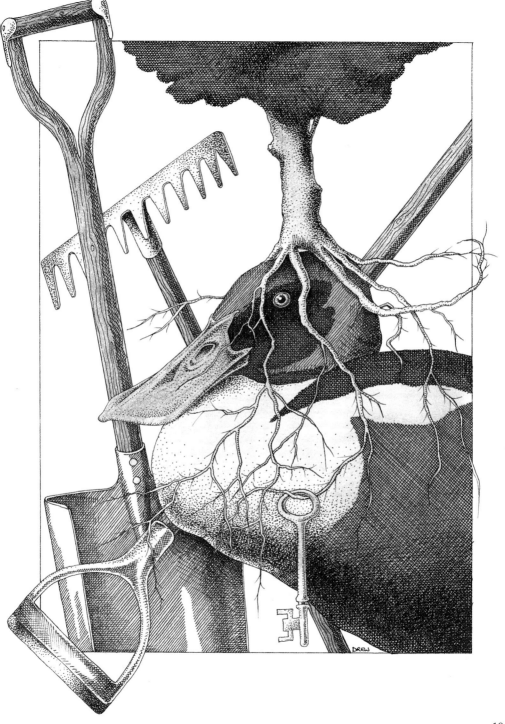

and when rooks and ravens
are wrapped up in string,

and woodpeckers whistle God Save the King,

and when there are gannets
that lecture in greek

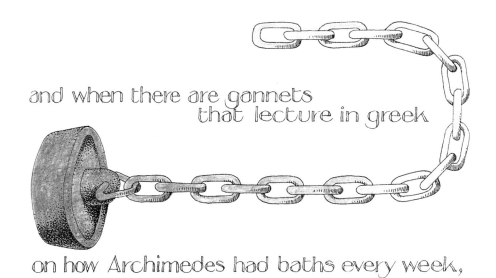

on how Archimedes had baths every week,

23

and when purple sandpipers wait to be shot,

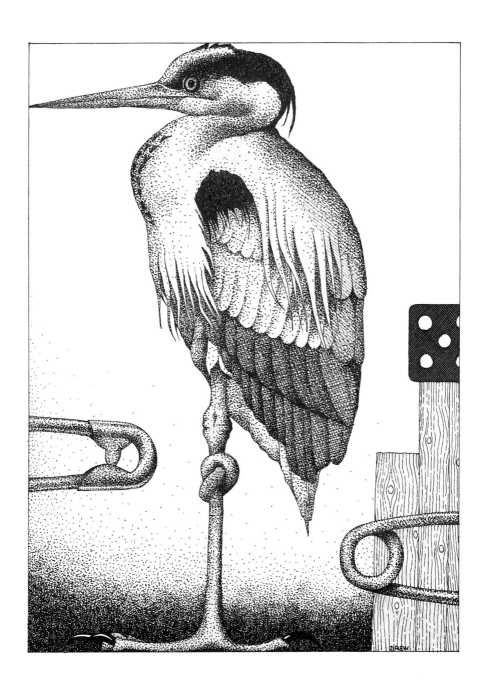

and herons have legs that are tied in a knot,

and when spotted parakeets sit on your phone
and ask if you're able to give them a loan,

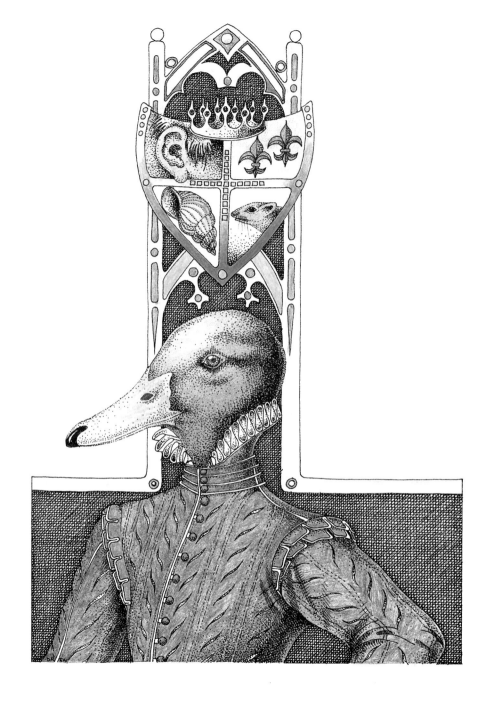

and when there's a mallard that claims it's an earl,

and nuthatches dive in the sea for a pearl,

and when you've forgotten to water your plants
but passing mergansers remind you by chance,

and when there are terns at the end of your garden
and vultures that belch have been taught to say pardon,

and when you see sparrows in deep conversation,

and cormorants laughing with no explanation,

and when there's a barnacle goose writing verse
while stood on its head like an underpaid nurse,

and when flapping doves can take men from their pockets,

and penniless gulls travel upwards on rockets,

and when there are emus in blazers and boaters
whose kneecaps are fitted with powerful motors,

and when you see wagtails that wink at a waiter,

and penguins that never say "Now," always "Later";

and when you find chickens with monstrous ambitions
of doing impressions of old politicians,

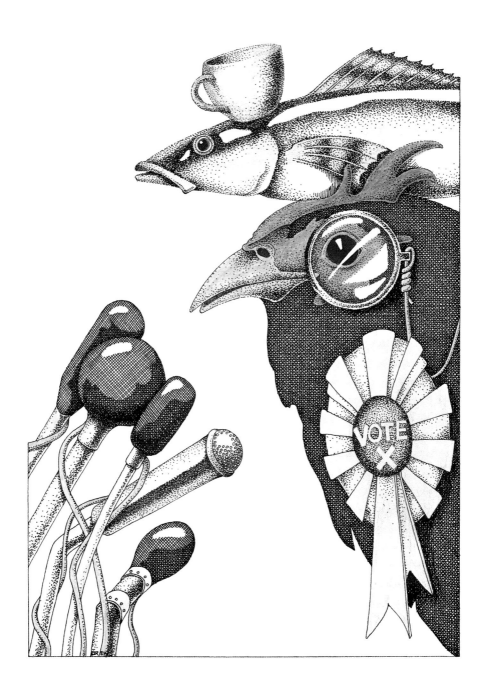

and when all the magpies
are too fat to carry
that is the time I advise you to marry."

the end

Postscript
The Puffin gave this advice because
either ⓐ he thought that no-one should
ever marry and so conjured up
impossible events,
or ⓑ he was under the firm
impression that any of these
things could happen at any
moment and so would be happy
to see the marriage.

Please yourself.

Other titles in this series.

A Book of
Bestial Nonsense
Simon Drew

Nonsense in Flight
Drawings and Verses by Simon Drew

Still Warthogs Run Deep
and other free range nonsense
Drawings and Verses by
Simon Drew

Simon Drew's previous volumes in this series have met with a rapturous reception. His elegant drawings of birds and beasts, combined with punning rhymes, comical prose, and verses full of imagination and fun, form a delightful collection. Gifted with a rare artistic talent, his superbly drawn wild life characters seem to inhabit a fantasy world unimagined by most casual observers. His interpretations of animal life, a unique mixture of the obvious and the unexpected, reveal a superbly inventive and highly amusing sense of humour. He has been described as a latterday Lewis Carroll and Edward Lear, and his topsy-turvy juxtaposition of words and pictures provide welcome relief from an otherwise grey world.